D0923601

STRAVINSKY
SEEN AND HEARD

STRAVINSKY
SEEN AND HEARD

HANS KELLER

and

MILEIN COSMAN

DA CAPO PRESS • NEW YORK • 1986

Library of Congress Cataloging in Publication Data

Keller, Hans, 1919–
    Stravinsky seen and heard.

    (Da Capo Press music reprint series)
    Reprint. Originally published: London: Toccata Press, 1982.
    Includes index.
    1. Stravinsky, Igo, 1882–1972. 2. Stravinsky, Igor, 1882–
1971 — Portraits, etc. I. Cosman, Milein. II. Title.
ML410.S932K4   1986   780'.92'4   84-17648
    ISBN 0-306-76264-1

    This Da Capo Press reprint edition of *Stravinsky Seen and Heard*
    is an unabridged republication of the first edition published
in London in 1982. It is reprinted by arrangement with Toccata Press.

Published by Da Capo Press, Inc.
A Subsidiary of Plenum Publishing Corporation
233 Spring Street, New York, N.Y. 10013

STRAVINSKY
SEEN AND HEARD

HANS KELLER

and

MILEIN COSMAN

Published by
TOCCATA PRESS
1982

First published in March 1982

© Hans Keller and Milein Cosman

Parts of this book first appeared in their *Stravinsky at Rehearsal*, Dobson
Books, London, 1962, and in *Tempo*, No. 35, London, 1955.

I would like to express my thanks to Messrs. Faber and Faber for permission
to quote from *Memories and Commentaries* by Igor Stravinsky and Robert
Craft. *H.K.*

British Library Cataloguing in Publication Data

Keller, Hans
  Stravinsky seen and heard.
  1. Stravinsky, Igor
  I. Title II. Cosman, Milein
  780'.92'4   ML410.S932

ISBN 0 907689 01 9 (cased edition)

ISBN 0 907689 02 7 (paperback edition)

Photoset in 11 on 12 point Baskerville and printed by Goron Pro-print
Co. Ltd., Lancing, W. Sussex.

Bound by Garden City Press Ltd., Letchworth, Herts.

Contents

PART ONE

STRAVINSKY HEARD

I. STRAVINSKY'S CHANGE OF MIND

Across the divisions of style, beyond the wars of musical 'schools', the rival symptoms and rival claims of creative inferiority feelings (unconfessed or at least semi-conscious); across all artificial curtains that separate the seeming irreconcilables of our disunited musical world, there cuts one straight division, the most recent and the most real of them all: the iron curtain between physical and phoney creativity. Not that the physical is the 'A' and 'O' of music; but it certainly is the 'A'.

The division was unimaginable so long as there were only musical composers. But once the crumbling of tonality had removed that common background, intuitively comprehensible in terms of sound alone, against which everybody composed, once backgrounds began to vary from composer to composer, making comprehension proportionately more difficult, the road was open to a confusion between the as yet uncomprehended and the necessarily incomprehensible — necessarily, inasmuch as it does not make sense as sound.

Today, we are quite often confronted with unmusical composers producing non-sounding sense; that they cheat their audiences is only incidental to their cheating themselves about their senseless sounds, which they themselves only 'understand' because they know the soundless sense behind, or rather beside the music. It gives birth to a great deal of notation which can't be heard, while sounding sense inevitably contains much that can't be notated. If the composers of downright unmusic are, of course, on the wrong side of the iron curtain, there are others whose very heart it tears asunder, with one half on the right side, the other under the dictatorship of soundless intellectualism, musically atrophied. They present the newest and greatest problem of musical culture, for some of our intensest talents are among them. There are only a handful whose heart is altogether pure, unharmed, untouched by the iron curtain which, with inexorable regularity, is drawn up for a fleeting moment and then crashes down again, hitting all but these very few.

Which few? For the duration of our musical crisis, a new, empirical criterion for the existence of genius seems to be emerging. It was only the geniuses amongst the composers writing in a twentieth-century idiom who retained their musicality uncorrupted, making sense of sound and of nothing else. They all belong to the recent past, where they may have made curious bedfellows — Schoenberg, Stravinsky, Britten, Skalkottas, Shostakovich — but even though they may not have known it, their hearts were united in sounding logic, and the sense behind their music (if you can so separate a sense that can only be musically expressed) is spiritual rather than intellectual — a message, revelation, or both, according to the character of the composer.

As time progresses, strange bedfellows get used to each other, not just through habit, but by discovering the affinities which made them bedfellows in the first place — or, if they do not live to see their unity, posterity sees it for them. One of my five geniuses, the father of our musical age, did not live to see the influence he was to exert on what he would have regarded as the most unlikely recipients of his thoughts — Britten and Stravinsky. His influence on Britten is relatively superficial, more psychological than musical, but in Stravinsky, Schoenberg's twelve-tone method eventually produced one of those profound changes of creative mind of which no other great creator, with the possible exception of Picasso, has ever been capable.

When Theodor Adorno, our age's musical philosopher-in-chief, wrote his *Philosophy of New Music* in 1949, he was still able to play off Schoenberg against Stravinsky, whose music he regarded as a death-mask of the past (my metaphor); in fact, the whole book develops in the field of tension created by the polarity Adorno postulated between Schoenberg and Stravinsky. Admittedly, at that stage, as indeed for decades before, the two composers represented the fundamental stylistic division of our age, and when I said at the time that they had something more basic in common than many Stravinskyians on the one hand and Schoenbergians on the other (to wit, music), my argument seemed tenuous: there were not many who shared my admiration for either composer. But then, in the twenties, more than two decades before I came in, a seemingly elemental historical clash had occurred: while Stravinsky, via neo-classicism, was diving into the past, Schoenberg, via the tone-row, was jumping into the future. So violent a contrast was too much for the composers themselves to bear: they theorized against each other, and though in later years they calmed down and re-realized that music was music, their ambivalent attitudes towards each other never quite left them.

How then, in the circumstances, was it possible for Stravinsky to turn serial in the fifties and sixties, at first cautiously and indeed tonally, later downright twelve-tonally and even atonally, making nonsense of Adorno's nowise senseless basic thesis? Even for an admirer of both composers, Stravinsky's absorption of Schoenberg's technique was arguably the profoundest surprise in the history of music.

With the help of psychological insight on the one hand and musical insight on the other, it should be possible to explain the late development of this most puzzling of all great composers — most puzzling because truly unprecedented.

All good composers start out from the past; they normally come to create against its background. Most bad composers remain stuck in it and are therefore compelled to use it as a foreground: to copy it. Stravinsky was the first great composer who had it both ways: he kept his past, or rather his pasts, in the glaring foreground, yet composed against them, or, if you like, through them. Anybody can twist a diatonic harmony, but only Stravinsky can re-characterize it by the addition of a wrong note or two.

Apropos of his treatment of Pergolesi's melodies in the ballet *Pulcinella* (1919-20), at that cataclysmic moment when he confronted Schoenberg across a wider and steeper precipice than any faced by any two artists at any time, Stravinsky asked: 'Should my line of action be dominated by my love or by my respect for Pergolesi's music? Is it love or respect that urges us to possess a woman? Is it not by love alone that we succeed in penetrating to the very essence of a being? But then, does love diminish respect? Respect alone remains barren and can never serve as a productive or creative factor. In order to create, there must be a creative force, and what force is more potent than love?' He felt his 'conscience to be innocent of sacrilege'; indeed, he considered that his attitude towards Pergolesi was 'the only possible one towards the music of earlier ages'. For 'love' read 'hate' without excluding love: we shall see at once precisely why.

We recall Stravinsky's suggestion that 'rape may be justified by the creation of a child'. Paul Valéry changed the metaphor: 'A lion consists of digested lambs'. Now, psychoanalysis recognizes two basic types of love, self-love apart. Genetically the more primitive is identification, which stems from the earliest, sucking stage of infancy and whose prototype is oral incorporation — hence the technical term 'introjection' for the 'absorption of the environment into the personality' (Ernest Jones); hence, too, Valéry's metaphor. The other type, 'object-love', is what we commonly understand by love. In monosyllables, identification is based on the need to *be* someone, object-love on the need to *have* someone. Identification, more primitive, is the more ambivalent of the two, the more aggressive: for one thing you destroy what you eat, for another you want to replace the person you want to be.

Ordinary artistic development always starts with identification: while the composer's own creative ego is still weak, he identifies himself with his teachers and with older masters, and proceeds to imitate them. This is the stage where the past, his future background, is still in the foreground of his creative thought. As his originality grows with the maturation of his creative personality, those father figures are absorbed by his artistic conscience and recede into the background. Once maturity is reached, and if no creative trauma lies in wait for him (such as the encounter with Bach which Mozart had to face as a mature genius), his creative 'love relations' with other composers amount to no more than sporadic flirtations resulting in, say, variations on another composer's theme: these are the children of 'object-love' rather than of identification.

Alone amongst geniuses, again with the possible exception of Picasso, Stravinsky actually developed his capacity for identification together with the unfolding of his intense originality. At the same time, as his commentary on *Pulcinella* indicates, his creative mind also employed a good deal of highly aggressive 'object-love' ('rape may be justified by the creation of a child'): he made the aggressive best of both love worlds, though identification remained the basic 'creative force'. No previous composer has shown any desire to compose his way 'into the very essence of a being'.

> And all men kill the thing they love,
>   By all let this be heard,
> Some do it with a bitter look,
>   Some with a flattering word,
> The coward does it with a kiss,
>   The brave man with a sword!

There is some special pleading here, but there is a truth too. Stravinsky did in fact himself employ the bitter look, the flattering word, and the sword, but he never killed the past by kissing it, as so many of his followers and all pure neo-classicists did.

Consider such a spotless and gigantic masterpiece as the *Symphony of Psalms* (1930), where identifications with the past span a wide field, stretching back into the archaic: when the opening four-part fugue of the second movement (with the answer in the dominant) raises its voice through what we might call the life-mask of Bach, we realize that the term 'neo-classicism' is no longer good enough — and in Chapter II we shall, at the bottom of it all, unearth the fugue subject's surprising, profound modernism.

Psychologically, the chief fascination of the *Symphony of Psalms* is the nature of its incisive expressiveness. That is to say, the work is expressive through the very suppression of expressionism, through that in-turned, self-castigating aggression which prompted Adorno and myself, independently, to describe it as sado-masochistic. I have been heavily criticized for this characterization; my simple reply is that it is not a devaluation. What it does signify is the complexity of Stravinsky's creative aggression, which manifests itself in his aggressive love and aggressive self-love. Stravinsky's genius utilized its sado-masochism, i.e. both its aggression turned inwards and its enjoyment of such self-attack, towards his unique, tense, meaning-laden suppressionism. His anti-expressionism did not, however, as Adorno thought, result in emptiness, but in fullness fully opposed, in a state of statically intense tension, of dynamic staticism.

The outstanding common trait of Stravinsky's successive styles is indeed their self-restrictive tendency. In point of fact, his urge towards formal stringency and simplicity might well be considered to go beyond the requirements of unity and clarity: he did not discipline his inspiration; rather, he was more lavishly inspired by self-discipline than any other composer before or even after him, when creators, robbed of universally valid disciplines and afraid of their undesired freedom, have tended to be obsessed with self-disciplinary measures as a matter of pathological course. The source of Stravinsky's self-restrictiveness was not only his in-turned aggression, but also his need for creative identification: identifications with other styles automatically impose severe limitations upon the imagination.

It is in the light of this psychological background, then, that Stravinsky's amazing change of mind towards serialism has to be examined. Now, the simplest, and perhaps the most important fact about his gradual conversion is its chronology: it all happened after Schoenberg's death — we might almost say, by way of creative mourning. Ever since 1916, when Freud published his *Mourning and Melancholia,* we have come to understand that what he called the 'identification of the ego with the lost object' is at the root of all mourning: in concentrated fashion, that very process of 'introjection' takes place which, as we have seen, forms part and parcel of Stravinsky's creative character anyhow.

Grief-inspired incorporations, once our attention is drawn

to them, are readily observable by the naked eye. They are especially impressive where the mourned person was a creative or public figure with well-defined, widely familiar character traits: we can all think of more than one widow who was inwardly compelled to burden her psyche with her great or famous husband's peculiarities, however eccentric, and to act out what she understood to be his role; right at the centre of the present essay's world, Mrs Schoenberg was a textbook example. Even on a social scale, the phenomenon makes itself easily felt when a personality dies whose work is hotly contested: public reactions veer in his favour, he is accepted as 'one of us', and unfavourable critics 'introject' him to the extent of turning into advocates. In fact, in the case of Schoenberg himself, while we who had always pleaded for his music prided ourselves on the eventual success of our endeavours, there is little doubt that when it came to it, psychology achieved what we hadn't. A comparison between some of our leading critics' writings before and after his death makes downright grotesque reading: an imaginary public was chided for the critic's own past attitudes.

Stravinsky's character having been predestined to identifications with, incorporations of the past, it is not, perhaps, quite so mysterious any longer that he naturally availed himself of the mourning mechanisms as soon as Schoenberg had become a thing of the past. At the same time, we must, I think, beware of facile explanations: the psychological situation is not as simple as all that. For one thing, why should Stravinsky mourn Schoenberg anyway? A condition of mourning is a fairly high minimum of love, the aggressive side of the picture being usually hidden from superficial inspection. With Stravinsky, on the other hand, we need not seek for the aggression; it is the love aspect of which we cannot find much trace. There is no positive evidence that deep love was lost between the two composers; when they landed in Hollywood, they did not venture near each other. In a sense, they must have disliked each other more generously than some music critics disliked both of them, for they were, after all, composers of diametrically opposite orientation, with a corresponding creative intensity behind their mutual dislike. Assuming, however, that there was more mutual love or respect than met the eye (and there is some evidence of suppressed admiration), the proportionate guilt reaction on Schoenberg's death would help Stravinsky towards that state of creative mourning. But it wouldn't be enough. Our psychological budget is still unbalanced; our explanation remains artificial so long as we do not find further items on the credit side of Stravinsky's most revolutionary identification, be they purely psychological, musical, or both.

Facts are better than theories, and nothing is more foolish than not to be wise after the event. Let us look at the precise nature and circumstances of Stravinsky's introjection of Schoenberg's method, as well as at his own attitude towards his change of direction, in order to discover more concretely how it came about. The first thing that strikes us, however, is a further element of confusion, a further inconsistency. Whereas, especially in their early stages, Stravinsky's serial ventures were stressedly Schoenbergian in technical approach, his public utterances almost throughout exalted Webern at the expense of Schoenberg, the implication being that he actually 'had it' from Webern, the real father of the future — a status still accorded to this great minor master by a substantial section of *avant-gardist* opinion which, in reality, is so rigidly old-fashioned that it hasn't changed at all in the course of more than a quarter-century. To my mind, this contradiction reached its manifest climax on a private occasion. In the early stages of Stravinsky's serial technique, when the news had reached the musical world that he admired Webern enormously, I wrote an article for *Tempo* (No. 35, 1955), entitled '*In Memoriam Dylan Thomas*: Stravinsky's Schoenbergian Technique', and containing a complete analysis of his Dylan Thomas dirge. Explicitly and implicitly, I showed that the strictly serial piece, though based on a five-note row, applied Schoenberg's own serial concept very conscientiously.

Now, the reader whose analytic interest in music is limited and who is not specifically preoccupied with the workings of serial technique need not really be bothered with the concrete details of that article, whereas the musicianly reader would not easily forgive me if I kept them from him — especially in view of Stravinsky's subsequent reaction to them. We can easily have it both ways: the next 10 paragraphs, together with the ensuing 5 pages of music type, need not be read; they reproduce my article and analysis in full.

*   *   *   *   *

Music examples usually illustrate verbal texts, but the present article is no more than an illustration appended to my analytic music example of the complete central song from Stravinsky's *In Memoriam Dylan Thomas* (Spring, 1954). I think that writers on music should be encouraged to keep to the music, and seriously contend that all the adverse critics of Schoenberg's serial technique, and most of the writers who pass for serial experts, are incapable of a serial analysis and have only the very vaguest notion of what makes a serial piece tick. They quote a bar or two — usually from the opening of Schoenberg's 4th Quartet — where the note-row is fairly obvious or, anyway, has previously been uncovered by someone else, and then proceed to let obscure theory take the place of clear if complex practice. The reason is simple: they don't hear the row, and if you are unable to imagine a row aurally, it is very difficult, usually indeed impossible, to trace it throughout a piece. Let me hasten to add that I should not dream of reproaching any critic with his tone-row-deafness if he left it at that: for all we know, he may otherwise be a musical genius. If, however, he professes to talk serial 'shop' at the same time, I raise the strongest moral objections.

The result of all this pseudo-articulate obscurantism has been catastrophic, in that the legend has developed that serial technique is something visual, something which could but need not be worked out on paper. Performers do not dream of acquainting themselves with a note-row of a serial piece, and even if they dreamt of it they would rarely be able to do something about it, because there is nobody to tell them that the music is written in serial technique, as for instance in the work under review. A state of performing affairs ensues which is as satisfactory as diatonic conditions would be if executants were unable to imagine the tonic of a piece they were performing.

In these circumstances, only the most supreme artists instinctively surmount their innocent ignorance. At Donaueschingen in 1954, for example, Peter Pears gave a masterly and indeed overwhelming performance of the Dylan Thomas song. When, after the concert, I remarked that the work was written in the strictest serial technique, he seemed amazed; in fact, in his mind serial methods seemed to be bound up with absolute atonality. Why did I enlighten him? Even Peter Pears could profit. He had sung the first note a semitone flat. He could not have done so if he had known the row.

Apart from such important practical and specific purposes, the present analysis is intended to give a concrete idea of the nature of serial technique itself. Stravinsky's canonic masterpiece is more suitable for this purpose than any work of Schoenberg's, because it applies the method far more strictly and, at the same time, more simply, primitively (no evaluation, this!) than Schoenberg's music ever did; besides, the application is only melodic, not harmonic, which makes things simpler for a start, since the harmonic aspect of serial technique is its most problematic. In most other respects, Stravinsky out-Schoenbergs Schoenberg, even though his is a five-note row which functions in a vaguely tonal fashion. The tonality of the piece would not, however, be enough to hold it together; in fact, some of Schoenberg's twelve-note music is more tonal than this piece. Nevertheless, since he does not, in principle, care about atonality, Stravinsky disregards one single serial directive, namely what Schoenberg calls 'avoidance of doubling in octaves'. I have marked octave doublings (a) in the refrain 'Rage, rage against the dying of the light', as well as at *Fig. 1*, in order to account serially for certain notes which do not, in one and the same part, form a complete row; and (b) in the last appearance of the opening ritornello (round *Fig. 10*) which, joined by the voice for the first time, shows dodecaphony's typical octave transpositions in the cello part. Throughout the song, Stravinsky freely avails himself of this variational device of Schoenberg's technique.

'BS' means Basic Set, 'R' Retrograde Version, 'I' Inversion, and 'RI' Retrograde Inversion. As with Schoenberg, different characters are derived from the basic set: its initial rhythm remains functional, but is not the lasting property of the series itself, which therefore is a real, sub-thematic, pre-rhythmic *row*, not a *theme*: a glance at *Fig. 3*, for instance, shows how rhythmic and motivic entities cut across the set and its mirror forms. Significantly enough, Stravinsky adopts Schoenberg's atonical practice of not repeating any notes of the row until all the notes are 'over', unless they are immediately or ornamentally repeated.* Other more individual traits of Stravinsky's serial technique, such as varying overlappings and intervals between successive series produced by various transpositions of the row, will be evident from a study of my analysis. Maximal overlapping can be observed in the tenor part in the first, third (*Fig. 7*) and last 'Do not go gentle into that good night': transposedly speaking, the last three notes of the inversion are identical with the first three of the retrograde version, and the last three of the basic set with the first three of the retrograde inversion.

The second 'Do not go gentle . . .' (before *Fig. 4*), on the other hand, shows the opposite of overlapping — stretching, if you like. The tenor's C flat on '-ning' is sustained across the parts (C flat in the 'cello followed by B in the viola) while the words 'they Do' double two notes from the 'cello's series (retrograde inversion and retrograde version), one of them in anticipation; after this parenthesis the tenor resumes the C flat that has been kept alive for him by the lower instruments. In other words, the 'cello's C flat quotes from the tenor, whereupon the tenor's A and A flat quote from

---

*As indeed he had done in the *Symphony of Psalms*: the purpose, then, is not exclusively atonical, but includes a sharper definition of the row *qua* row.

the 'cello. At the same time, the tenor's 'they Do not' is the middle part of a retrograde row whose first and last notes are the 'cello's B flat on '-ning' (preceding bar) and the viola's C on 'not' respectively. Serially, this is the most complicated passage. The only other irregularity, after *Fig. 6*, is much simpler: taking up the tenor's C, the 'cello's supernumerary C and the ensuing serial oscillation are made possible and, in fact, partially motivated by the canon between the tenor and the first violin, wherein two successive transpositions of the inversion yield three descending semitones followed by an ascending semitone, with the third semitone belonging to a new rhythmic articulations: the 'cello's oscillating motifs are likewise based on three descending semitones, two of them forming a rhythmic unit and sequential model. In the further course of this retrograde version, Stravinsky once more employs the one dodecaphonic device from which he refrains elsewhere in the work — the distribution of the row's notes between the parts: see the D flat in the first violin two bars before *Fig. 7*. The note is obviously over-determined, for at the same time it is part of a linear inversion. There is nothing exceptional in this: all the notes in the horizontal overlappings between the four variants of the row, are, of course, over-determined.

A day or two before writing this note, I talked to one of our leading composers who had examined the present work. He proved utterly unaware of its technique. I thereupon decided to keep my observations as elementary as possible, at the risk of disappointing serial experts. My analysis, however, should make it easy for them to study the many finer points of Stravinsky's application of the serial method.

As for my analytic brackets themselves, where two series overlap by way of repeated closing and opening notes respectively, I have, on the whole, indicated the widest extent of overlapping. In one or two instances, however, I have departed from this practice for extraneous reasons, e.g., spatial convenience. These divergencies are quite unimportant and of no musical significance.

The song here analysed is a setting of the poem which Dylan Thomas wrote in memory of his father, and forms the middle section of a ternary build whose outer sections consist of purely instrumental 'dirge-canons' that alternate between four trombones and string quartet. In Schoenbergian fashion, the entire work is based on a single row. In the outer sections, however, the row is rhythmically committed, overtly thematic. In consequence, the Pre- and Postlude analyse themselves as it were, yet Stravinsky marks the 'Theme', 'Inversion' and so on throughout the Prelude. In the song itself, on the other hand, i.e., at the very moment when the old contrapuntal technique crystallizes into the new serial method, where the theme becomes a row and will not therefore be heard or seen as a matter of course, Stravinsky's brackets cease. Why, in that case, he has bothered to analyse the first section is incomprehensible.* At the same time, it is somewhat depressing to find that the five successive notes of the opening theme seem to remain unrecognized as soon as they go underground. There is a limit to unconscious understanding.

After so much objective criticism, I may be allowed to add that I consider this new work Stravinsky's greatest and most perfect since the *Mass*: it is more coherent than the Septet and establishes stronger contrasts than the preceding Cantata.

---

*Stravinsky subsequently explained: 'In correcting the proofs I forgot to erase in the prelude these brackets left over from my final sketches, where they were put throughout the work, this complicating the reading of the instrumental and vocal score'.

SONG

Do not go gentle*

*The text is taken from *The Collected Poems of Dylan Thomas,* Dent, London, 1952.

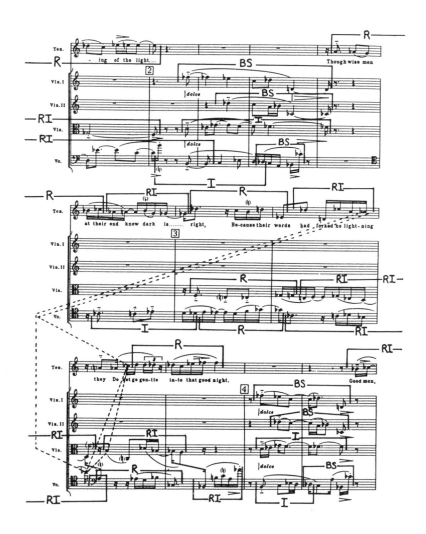

Now, for reasons which need not concern us here but of which I approved, the then editor of *Tempo* sent a proof of the article to the composer before it was published. It came back with stressedly appreciative, wholly confirmatory marginal comments, and without a word of criticism. At the same time, on more public occasions, Stravinsky made his indebtedness to Webern ever clearer — and his ambivalence towards Schoenberg too. There are passages in Robert Craft's *Conversations with Igor Stravinsky* which make one seriously wonder whether the composer really had a proper look at all the Schoenberg works he criticizes (he certainly cannot have heard them all), though in order to keep his ambivalence as tidy as possible in his difficult psychological circumstances, he reserves his most whole-hearted and general condemnation for Schoenberg's literary output: 'Schoenberg's work has too many inequalities for us to embrace it as a whole. For example, nearly all of his texts are apallingly bad, some of them so bad as to discourage performance of the music.' As a matter of fact, German-speaking countries acknowledged Schoenberg's great literary gifts decades before they recognized his musical genius; while nowadays, his texts are even appreciated by foreigners, by critics within Stravinsky's own cultural orbit: 'What is so striking [about *Moses and Aron*] is the enormous significance of the libretto and its unusual form. This text is concentrated to an extreme degree. Psychologically as well as dramatically and ethically, it is of a compactness which we never encounter in the realm of opera. There is no padding here, there are none of the *clichés* with which operatic texts commonly abound . . . It is a fact that Schoenberg has found a remarkable balance between the literary and the musical elements of his work.' Thus Claude Rostand.

But while Stravinsky's opinions of Schoenberg oscillated between extremes, Webern couldn't put a foot wrong — be it Webern the composer or Webern the man. In fact, Stravinsky's eulogy on Webern in the second batch of conversations between him and Robert Craft (*Memories and Commentaries*) prompted Peter J. Pirie to the somewhat despairing observation that he could not make up his mind 'about the exact intellectual stature of a man who . . . sentimentalizes like a teenager over Webern . . .'. I dislike this kind of description of a genius's reaction to a master, however minor, but the very fact that a by no means insensitive critic was driven to it is an indication of the intensity and purity of

Stravinsky's admiration for Webern. There is only one parallel, an acutely striking one, to this kind of public propaganda, on the part of a genius, for a dead master: Schoenberg's own memorial lecture on Gustav Mahler (1912), translated and reprinted in *Style and Idea*. The history of Schoenberg's relation to Mahler is itself one of passionate ambivalence, and the lecture is a guilt reaction if ever there was one, 'mourning and melancholia' *par exellence*.

What I had to introduce as an element of confusion, the seemingly impenetrable cloud hanging over Stravinsky's 'true' feelings about Schoenberg and Webern, seems to turn into the first step towards the solution of our problem. My metaphor is carefully mixed: the cloud is substantial, solid; we may step on it and look beyond. The fact is that all feelings are 'true', and if they contradict each other they are all the truer, stronger: if either side isn't strong, it gives in and is liquidated. Stravinsky's unconscious was prepared to incorporate and mourn Schoenberg on condition that Webern could be absorbed at the same time, and that the manifestly aggressive side of the psychological deal could be confined to Schoenberg, so that Webern could bathe in Schoenberg's glory as well as his own.

Our next and final two steps seem now clearly marked. We have to find out what made it possible for Stravinsky to be attracted by Webern to such an extent, and what made it necessary to retain Schoenberg.

Now it so happens that apart from Stravinsky himself, Webern is the only great sado-masochistic figure in the history of music. In his case, masochism and in-turned sadism are markedly stronger than in Stravinsky's; self-restrictiveness turns into self-destruction. What I mean is that Webern had been misunderstood by his followers with such absolute consistency that we must make him at least partly responsible for this historical, and by now historic misapprehension: it is as if he had worked towards being killed after his death. Much of the prestige of his work amongst composers depends in fact on the suppression of that which it expresses or purports to express, namely, emotion. Urged on by his masochism, Webern drove his heart-felt *espressivo* style beyond the extremes of compression towards partial or sometimes wholesale suppression. With Stravinsky, such suppression is suppressionism: it is artistically intended and hence functional, i.e. itself expressive. With Webern it is unintentional, accidental from the artistic point of view, though essential psychologically. In that sense, Webern's art is pathological, neurotic, whereas Stravinsky's isn't. Neurosis is unrealism; in art, it is a failure of adjustment to psychic reality. Inasmuch as Webern did not say what he had to say and what he thought he was saying, and inasmuch as this was not due to technical deficiencies (which, in my view, it virtually never was), he was a neurotic master (the only one in our history apart from Brahms, who tended to deny his feelings when he became afraid of them, fearing them to be 'sentimental').

It can easily be seen how Stravinsky was gladly prepared to swallow (incorporate) this sado-masochistic character — so long as he did not have to swallow it whole. Let us be a little more concrete and turn to the musical effects of Webern's sado-masochism — his sparse, ultra-transparent textures, cleaner, it must be said, than anything our entire musical history had had to offer until then. Once Stravinsky was incorporating the twelve-tone method, which itself offers many self-restrictive possibilities to those (and only to those) who want them, once his hostility towards atonality was on the wane, Webern's textures must have exercised a particular fascination on the suppressionist: it is one of the supreme paradoxes of musical history, as indeed of history in general, that pathology can produce health. (The opposite, alas, is also true, as can be observed in the Nazi interpretations of Wagner, Nietzsche, and even Bruckner.) If Webern was ever capable of musical development — in healthy circumstances one of the inevitable consequences of an *espressivo* style — his sado-masochism soon drove the capacity out of his system; and Stravinsky, the anti-expressionist and professed anti-developer *par excellence*, must have been happy to hear the unfinished result — unfinished because the twelve-tone method, a developmental procedure if ever there was one, suppresses itself in Webern's work. How Stravinsky managed to use the method undamaged, yet undeveloping, remains one of the miracles of genius; but one thing is certain — that he could not have done so without, on the one hand, his absolute loyalty to physical musical reality, to sounding sense, and on the other (or not so other) hand, Schoenberg's help.

We thus come to the last step in our investigation. When everything psychological is said and done, what was it in Schoenberg's own twelve-tone method that attracted Stravinsky so intensely and lastingly that it made all the psychological complications we have described worthwhile? And even on the assumption of a topically favourable psychological climate such as I have outlined, of potent stimuli towards identification exciting this perpetually identifying creative character, what was it, musically, that overcame a lifetime of musical resistance, an era of official musical polarity? Had Stravinsky 'killed the thing he loved', had he treated Schoenberg's twelve-tone method as savagely as Webern treated his own, our explanation would not be far to seek; it could, in fact, remain on the psychological level. But he didn't. On the contrary, with the exception of Nikos Skalkottas and the partial exception of Roberto Gerhard, Schoenberg's method has not, to date, found as realistic a follower as Stravinsky.

So far, when speaking about twelve-tone technique, I have kept my remarks general, hoping that they would so make essential sense to the uninitiated, while the versed would pin them down to the relevant concrete details. But when explaining Schoenberg's specific attraction for Stravinsky, I shall have to be mildly technical, without, however, saying anything that presupposes a great deal of technical knowledge.

While for Webern the tone-row is usually abstract, which is to say that it does not readily crystallize into something of melodic significance and therefore remains largely inaudible, the Schoenbergian tone-row is *abstracted from a melodic idea*, an initial inspiration: by and large, it *is* this idea without its rhythm — a succession of notes derived from a tune, and uncommitted to the rhythm of the tune: my term for it is 'sub-thematic'. It may be a little longer than the tune, in which case the rest of the row may be used towards the continuation; or it may be a bit shorter than the tune, in which case the tune will comprise more than one rotation of the row. In any case, however, the characteristic trait of the Schoenbergian row is its original concreteness — its function as a melodic motif, retaining its melodic aspect even when it is divested of its rhythm, or rather, when endowed with a new rhythm. It is due to the melodic idea from which it springs, and the melodic quality which it therefore retains, that the Schoenbergian row is ultimately and spontaneously audible. As Chapters II and III will hope to show, the musical importance of such concreteness and audibility cannot be overrated, nor has it yet been fully appreciated.

The vast majority of serial composers evince exactly the opposite approach, to which Webern inclined, which he was even the first to practise — without, however, fully subscribing to it. With them, the serial idea, the idea of a particular series or a special kind of series, comes first, and the music afterwards. The more pronouncedly phoney ones among them have even gone so far as to write of Schoenberg's rows contemptuously as 'music-making rows' (*Musizierreihen*), comparing them unfavourably with their own 'structural' rows. I cannot explain to the reader what exactly a 'structural' row is, or why it is more structural than a 'music-making' row, because I have never understood the term myself; suffice it to say that you don't know a structural row when you hear it.

However, what drew Stravinsky to Schoenberg's method, despite the vast difference in compositorial outlook between the two, was, I suggest, its 'music-making' significance. Again and again, I used to point to this, as it seemed to me, obvious trait of Stravinsky's serial technique, long before he did so himself. When he finally did (in *Memories and Commentaries*), he made no mention, of course, of Schoenberg, but the way in which he described his technique left no more doubt about the correctness of my diagnosis. The crucial passage runs as follows:

> Robert Craft: Would you analyse your own composing process in any part of one of your more recent pieces — in, for example, the little *Epitaphium*?
>
> Stravinsky: I began the *Epitaphium* with the flute-clarinet duet . . . In the manner I have described in our previous conversations I heard and composed a melodic-harmonic phrase. I certainly did not (and never do) begin with a purely serial idea and, in fact, when I began I did not know, or care, whether all twelve notes would be used. After I had written about half the first phrase I saw its serial pattern, however, and then perhaps I began to work towards that pattern. The constructive problem that first attracted me in the two-part counterpoint of the first phrase was the harmonic one of minor seconds.

Compare this with Schoenberg's categorical statement in a letter to Josef Rufer (quoted in the latter's *Composition with Twelve Notes*; the translation is mine): 'The original idea of a row always occurs to me in the form of a thematic character'.

The road to our understanding is clear. Across the divisions of style, beyond the wars of their schools, Stravinsky and Schoenberg eventually met on the basis of concrete, audible, sounding sense. By way of creative mourning, Stravinsky, who had always tended towards ambivalent identification, became aware of the concrete possibilities in Schoenberg's method and proceeded to incorporate it, insisting on getting Webern into the bargain. With the unerring certainty of genius, he split his mourning attitude between the two composers (some of his remarks about Webern sound as if the Schoenberg pupil had died yesterday) and took from either what he needed, leaving the unrealistic aspects of Webern as well as the developmental and expressionist aspects of Schoenberg on one side. Fascinated, yet uncorrupted, by some of the most recent, partly un-sounding developments of musical composition, he continued to make sense of sound and of nothing else, an advanced aim to those whom even he regarded as more advanced than himself. Look after the physical reality of your music, he told them and still tells them, and the spirit will look after itself. Unlike them, he is not an arm-chair composer; he remains what this book shows him to be — a music-maker.

II. STRAVINSKY'S UNCHANGED MIND

Two questions remain or arise, according to whether or not you share what you may regard as my prejudices — which I, however, consider severely tested working hypotheses: if you share them, these questions have been with you all along, at least on a pre-conscious level. In any case, each deserves a chapter on its own.

The first is burning — ablaze, in fact: convincing as our interpretation of Stravinsky's change of creative mind may be, how was it possible for a great creator to be capable of it all? Must we not agree with my hypothesis that whatever happens in the creative life of a genius, however surprising his metamorphoses, his diametrically opposed, successive creative attitudes may be to the outside observer, they will invariably be found to have profound determinants in his own psyche, palpable causes, tangible endo-psychic precedents which, though they must have remained latent until external stimuli produced the manifest change of mind, are an essential part of his creative character? A genius' revolution, in a word, must have an evolutionary aspect.

Come to think of it, is it not stunning that the critical fraternity, though preoccupied in conscientious detail with Stravinsky's sensational absorption of serial technique, has never yet as much as asked itself what, in the music preceding it, can be said to have led up to it? Twelve-tonery is, after all, a far- and deep-reaching way of musical thinking — which a mere talent may adopt, play with, 'use' without the underlying musical substance requiring this particular procedure, but which a genius would never as much as consider if his creative substance did not urge him towards it, if it did not, in fact, contain the seeds of serial technique itself. I thus accuse, above all, the Stravinskyians amongst critics, musicologists, and analysts, of not taking their idol seriously enough: how can they not wonder how it all happened, external stimulation apart, how Stravinsky's own mind had prepared for the event, without his being aware of the fact? When, in Chapter I, we examined Stravinsky's psychological budget and calculated 'the credit side of his revolutionary identifications', we naturally ignored this factor of an independent, internal incentive — not because we doubted its existence, but, on the contrary, because without it, any budgeting would have been senseless: it is not an item on the credit side, but the very condition for the opening of a credit account.

Those internal causes must, surely, always have formed an element in his composing methods, must have established themselves as a characteristic, concrete expressive means which, however unconscious to begin with, made the overt, conscious change of mind possible. Let's face it, either we can unambiguously show even the most anti-serial Stravinsky to have harboured, nevertheless, unconscious serial tendencies, or else we are confronted with the disconcerting alternative of having to deny him genius or ourselves insight — an inconceivable dilemma. Remembering, however, that Schoenberg himself composed with unconscious tone-rows long before he consciously discovered his twelve-tone technique, and that even the classical composers (yes, Beethoven, even Mozart) can be shown — as I demonstrated decades ago in great detail in a paper on 'Strict Serial Technique in Classical Music' (*Tempo*, No. 37, 1955) — to have practised Schoenberg's own technique without the remotest awareness of what they were doing, we need not feel grotesquely unrealistic, artificial rather than artistic, if we decide to examine or re-examine the passionately anti-Schoenbergian, neo-classical Stravinsky's methods of unification in an attempt to uncover downright serial thought processes — at the very stage in his development when his conscious mind ridiculed serial technique, and decades before he made dodecaphony his conscious own or, we may come to conclude, before Schoenberg's death allowed him to let his own serial inclinations emerge into consciousness.

The one neo-classical theme we have so far alluded to is the subject of the opening four-part fugue of the *Symphony of Psalms'* second movement, which we heard through the life-mask of Bach; had we listened a little more closely, or rather, a little more widely, thus perceiving the theme's integration with the entire work in general and the first movement in particular, we could have heard the life-mask of Schoenberg, too.

Or could we? Serial integration we can certainly diagnose very concretely, and with wellnigh traumatic surprise too, but there is no need, no reason to claim that at that early stage, Stravinsky 'had it' unconsciously from Schoenberg, who did not, after all, invent the method; he merely intellectually discovered and isolated and systematized a natural mode of musical thought that had been operative in many a masterpiece long before he was born.

In any event, so simple and straightforward is Stravinsky's unconscious application of the row technique in the present instance (or his conscious application of a technique of whose strictly serial nature he must, in that case, have been unaware) that despite the fact that the history of composition can hardly offer a greater technical sensation than a piece of essential, indispensable serialism in Stravinsky's greatest neo-classical masterpiece, the un-initiated reader is not, this time, invited to turn his back on our technical demonstration; on the contrary, Stravinsky will enlighten him, as he seemed to enlighten himself, about the very

nature and purpose of serial thinking. The concluding thought of
Schoenberg's only essay on twelve-tone technique ('Composition
with Twelve Tones', in *Style and Idea*) seems highly relevant at this
point:

> In music there is no form without logic, there is no logic without
> unity.
>
> I believe that when Richard Wagner introduced his *Leitmotiv* — for
> the same purpose as that for which I introduced my Basic Set* —
> he may have said: "Let there be unity".

If the reader remembers the *Symphony of Psalms* at all (a
greater, deeper work than which Stravinsky never created), he will
readily recall what I have isolated on the left-hand side of my
music example, i.e. the first movement's nowise concealed ac-
companiment which, I can now inform him, gives us a simul-
taneous double exposition of the 4-tone row — a basic set together
with its transposition — that serves to establish unity not only
within the movement, but actually between movements: the fugue
subject on the right-hand side is based on another transposition of

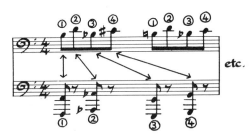

etc.

it, and on the transposition's rotations which, significantly enough,
behave exactly according to the twelve-tone rules formulated by
Schoenberg a few years earlier, and laughed at by Stravinsky's conscious mind — by what he and we then thought was Stravinsky.

Thus, the row is and remains totally independent of any of
its rhythmic articulations; it does not, in a word, remain a rhythmic
entity. Again, as in the case of the Dylan Thomas dirge, octave
transpositions do not adversely affect its identity, though the
melodic innovations they introduce are sufficiently drastic to hide
this very identity which, sub-thematically, produces the intensest

---

*Note to the virginal reader: the 'basic set' is the original (initial) form of the tone-row, as
distinct from its 'mirror forms' — the inversion, the retrograde version, and the retrograde
inversion.

unity between what thus become dissimilar shapes. Lastly, though
the context is, of course, tonal, the row's configuration is defined,
re-defined and thus maintained in vastly different harmonic
circumstances: there is no harmonic identity between whichever of
the two left-hand rows we choose to call the basic set and its two
transpositions.

I have extricated these particular occurrences and rotations
of the row in order to provide a quick and clear, yet comprehensive
example of Stravinsky's serial technique in the Symphony; a
complete analysis of its role in the unification of the work would, of
course, reach far further. But my example is, structurally, of central
significance, and for my part, I have no doubt that Stravinsky de-
liberately employed these successions of intervals and their
inversions; what he did not realize, and indeed, psychoanalytically
speaking, repressed, was the circumstance that through so acting,
and especially because of his extra-rhythmic, extra-diatonic
approach to his successions of intervals, he landed himself straight
in the strictest possible serial technique, albeit of as primitive a

type as Schoenberg himself had employed early on, in one of his
first consistently twelve-tonal structures (the fourth movement of
his Serenade, Op. 24, composed seven years before the *Symphony of
Psalms*). By 'primitive type' I simply mean the absence of any
mirror forms, such as inversion, retrograde, and retrograde
inversion, all of which the more specifically interested reader will
have found, or might now wish to revert to, in the Dylan Thomas
dirge.

We remember that much later, when Stravinsky had
consciously serial ideas, he 'did not know, or care, whether all
twelve notes would be used'. No wonder that when he began unconsciously, he didn't care either: Schoenberg himself hadn't cared
before his own serial technique reached his consciousness. The

twelve notes are, in fact, the only theoretical aspect of twelve-tone technique — the result, that is of the decision to unify without the help of tonality. They are, therefore, Schoenberg's only personal contribution to the method he discovered, its consistent application apart. At the same time, the *Symphony of Psalms'* four-note row is not the shortest possible: in the aforementioned essay on the classical twelve-toners, I showed that at the beginning of the development section of the finale from his famous G minor Symphony, Mozart uses a three-note row — and, ironically enough, lets it behave more anti-tonally than the maturest Schoenberg allows more than one of his twelve-tone rows to behave; that of the *Ode to Napoleon*, for instance, while starting anti-tonally, eventually contributes to a triumphant E flat conclusion.

It is abundantly obvious, then, that the serial mode of thought came quite naturally to Stravinsky — that he was able to practise it instinctively, with unconscious certainty about *what* had to be done, *how* things had to be done and how they could *not* be done if the row was to serve unification and, hence, comprehension; even Schoenberg's constructive negative rule is heeded as a matter of natural, instinctive course: none of the row's notes recurs after another one has been sounded, and before the row as a whole has unfolded.

I have suggested that Picasso was perhaps the only other great creator capable of comparably profound changes of mind — and I would now go further and submit that in his case, likewise, an 'unchanged mind' must eventually be demonstrable across even the most violent changes, each of which must needs have tapped latent, yet well developed and well-defined sources; it is, I humbly propose, up to my brothers-in-analytic-arms in the present book's other artistic world to find them — unless they have done so behind my back. The underlying assumption is, admittedly, that Picasso was a great creator, a genius, but while I am not entitled to pronounce upon visual art, it is my very ignorance through which the power of Picasso's genius cuts the way the downright elemental force of serial logic cut through Stravinsky's pseudo-elemental prejudices against it; mourning without melancholia killed them and freed it.

I was almost going to conclude this chapter by saying that any musician would be aghast if nobody had yet explored the endo-psychic determinants of Picasso's changes of mind — but then, which musician before the present one cared about Stravinsky's? I am indeed aghast that nobody did — unless the same resistances have been at work which kept Stravinsky's spontaneous serial thought firmly locked in the safe of his unconsciousness. After all, he himself couldn't find the key until after Schoenberg's death.

III. THE MUSIC-MAKER'S FUTURE

The other question which remains or arises in view of Stravinsky's change of mind flows from my working hypothesis that however conservative a genius may be or seem, his very genius will, inevitably, be of profound relevance to the future of his art — potentially and/or actually so: Bach and Mozart, for instance, were almost notoriously conservative geniuses, at least in the ears of many observers, contemporary observers (even composers) in the case of Bach, posthumous observers in the case of Mozart. Yet Schoenberg, for instance, regarded himself as a pupil of both Bach and Mozart, nor would it be difficult to show what he learnt from them. What, however, the historical investigator never considers is that part of a conservative genius' influence on the future which is or was destined to remain potential — the influence that never happened. We are, nevertheless, justified in calling it an influence if we can demonstrate that in certain circumstances beyond the genius' control, it could, should have happened.

Take Mozart, the greatest amongst his string quintets, at least four of them, on the one hand, his two piano quartets, his string trio (the so-miscalled 'Divertimento') and the two violin-viola duos on the other. Out of nothing, without any truly helpful precedent, he created supreme masterpieces in each of these media, some of which evince an originality of both structure and texture which can only be compared to the originality of the greatest string quartets of Haydn and Beethoven. Yet, while Haydn duly became the founder of the Austro-German string quartet and Beethoven its almost unreachable prophet, Mozart did not succeed in proving himself the founder or prophet of a comparable tradition in any of these areas of instrumental combinations. Why not? The traditions never really happened. Strictly speaking, his G minor Piano Quartet was to remain the only supreme masterpiece of its textural kind;* the two-viola quintet, likewise, never found its way back to Mozart's elevated level; the string trio, after Beethoven, had to wait until Schoenberg to throw up another great masterpiece; and the violin-viola duo never returned to Mozart's level of weighty mastery at all.

The point is that it can easily be shown why it wasn't Mozart's fault that things didn't happen; it was the fault of his successors, however great their genius. For as soon as we examine the different textures of these instrumental combinations, we find that unlike the string quartet, each of them harbours profound problems so far as their sheer sound is concerned, problems which needed a Mozartian ear in order to be either overcome or simply ignored. However, the historical fact is that after Mozart, there was no Mozartian ear – which, it will be admitted, wasn't his fault. Yet it is because there was no Mozartian ear after Mozart that we call him a conservative.

Or, very conscientiously and equally concretely speaking, there was one, almost — Mendelssohn's. After Mozart, that is to

---

*Though equally flawless, his other piano quartet, in E flat, makes life easier for itself as a texture, which is that of a mini piano concerto.

say, Mendelssohn's was the only ear capable of overcoming, or ignoring, most textural problems — situations, that is to say, which presented problems to all other composers — without even needing practical experience, practice: one would have thought that the texture of the *Midsummer Night's Dream* Overture, for instance, needed a lifetime's aural experience. Mendelssohn's inner ear, in a word, seemed indistinguishable from his physiological ear, in that his aural imagination differentiated as subtly as did his perception. But his genius, though towering, was not, of course, of Mozart's order. Nevertheless, he was not only the one composer after Schubert and before our own age whose quartet textures reached classical perfection, but also the only composer altogether who did actually continue what was the richest, most radical and, potentially, the most fruitful of Mozart's textural innovations — the two-viola string quintet: his two works in that medium are the only ones that bear comparison with Mozart's quintet textures, the only ones which show no sign of any problem existing. Without the Mozartian model, they would probably never have been created; and their musical substance, too, proves them his worthy successors — so that in this single respect, at least, it is difficult to consider him an uninitiating conservative. There are two other respects — the string trio (Beethoven, Schoenberg) and, over-ridingly, the piano concerto: what would have happened to, and about the piano concerto without Mozart? We tend to forget both what had happened, or rather hadn't, before he came in with his unprecedented masterpieces, and what did happen to Beethoven as a result of them. No matter, what is of crucial importance in our present context is a concrete understanding of Mozart as a *potential* innovator, for actual *or* potential innovation is, according to a working hypothesis which the majority of readers will share, inseparable from the phenomenon of genius, one of its *conditiones sine qua non*.

Stravinsky is, of course, our age's conservative genius *par excellence*. Britten would indeed be another, but does not occupy a polar position *via-à-vis* our age's revolutionary *par excellence* — and the fact that Stravinsky came to adopt the latter's revolutionary methods does not detract from his conservatism: he came to conserve them, too. His actual influence on that part of the future which has, meanwhile, become present is nothing or little to write home about: there is Britten as a recipient, of course, but that's about it, for all the many remaining results of Stravinsky's influence are nothing short of deplorable, and easily descend to the film-musical plane of kitschy anti-kitsch — suppressionism without anything to suppress. Nor indeed is it easy to imagine that Stravinsky's various, contrasting conservatisms will be capable of exerting a fruitful influence on any future creativity — with the sole exception of his last and most surprising act of conservatism, that revolutionary, yet evolutionary change of mind which produced the conservation of Schoenberg's, yet also Stravinsky's characteristic method.

'Characteristic' is the doubly operative word: the 'music-making row' is characteristically Schoenberg's, and as both Stravinsky said and we showed in Chapter II, it was the only way in which he himself could think serially, as opposed, very much opposed, to the serial *and* extra-serial thinking of the vast majority of anti-conservative contemporary composers, all of them well on the other side of Chapter I's iron curtain. As an observer whose professional activities have involved him in familiarizing himself with the widest conceivable variety of contemporary scores, I give it as my empirical opinion that at the present, critical juncture in the development of composition, even considerable talents find themselves, under the pressure of influential, 'advanced' forces, on the other side of the iron curtain; and that nowadays, it needs not only deep musicality, but also sheer moral strength to remain on, or defect to, this side, Stravinsky's.

The question of his influence on the future is amongst the most difficult with which genuinely musical criticism can concern itself at the end of the twentieth century — because we now have to face two phenomena for which there is no precedent, phenomena which lie outside musical history, if history is the story of the same causes producing the same effects. The phenomenon of Stravinsky's own creative personality is without the remotest parallel: Picasso may be a comparable mind-changer, but he is not a suppressionist, nor is there any sign of Stravinsky's suppressionism as such being capable of exerting a favourable influence. So far, in fact, this influence has proved a mere, powerful excuse for saying nothing — a pseudo-creative activity which is more popular nowadays than it ever was. Quite often a contemporary composer will have met the demands of his conscience if, instead of saying something, he makes absolutely clear what he is not going to say, what he feels aggressive about — what, in his view, is improper artistic behaviour. Not seldom with Stravinsky's help, he will have accumulated a bunch of anti-sentimental gestures, of ruthless ostinatos, of spiced-up, unfunctional demi-semi-diatonic harmonies which will inform the listener to which camp the composer does not belong; such an introductory exposition of the composer's premises will easily prove so enjoyable to the composer that it will soon lose its introductoriness and replace the creative act altogether: again for the first time in the history of music, it has become possible, permissible, even reputable, to say what one is against and leave it at that. In both composition and performance, avoidance poses as art. Stravinsky's unique personality as such, then, cannot foreseeably exert an auspicious influence on his successors — or if it can, it is too unique for us to be able to divine the unforeseeable. Schoenberg's uniqueness is a very different story: its traceable relations to Beethoven's uniqueness have made it possible for us to foresee his influence in terms of Beethoven's, even though the historical situations surrounding the two could hardly be more dissimilar.

Which brings us to the other phenomenon without precedent – our present historical situation, or rather, often conflicting situations, whose complexity and complications seem to be reaching their extended climax at the end of the century: in comparison, what surrounded and immediately succeeded Schoenberg was historical simplicity itself. Mind you, he had indeed started it all, in that the total abandonment of tonality paved the way not only for unmusicality in the guise of atonal incomprehensibility, but also for the replacement of creation with game-playing: where there are no rules, the mere definition of, and subsequent adherence to new rules feels like a creative achievement, to both the composer and his ever more un-aural audience; those new rules, as opposed to the *a posteriori* rules of diatonic harmony, need the eye rather than the ear in order to be understood and followed, and in order for such following to be understood.

Am I talking, amongst many others, about twelve-tone rules? That depends on the individual twelve-tone row you have in mind. One and the same rule, that is to say, will be easily audible when applied to a row of Schoenberg's, or Skalkottas', or

Stravinsky's, but exclusively visible when applied to most other people's. In Chapter I, we have drawn attention to the legend of serial technique being visual. Unfortunately, the legend becomes reality where the music is a mere phantom, albeit a highly successful one. It is in view of Schoenberg's or Stravinsky's serial technique that one can safely speak of a legend; but then, most of our current historical situations have become unsafe, sundry visual games lending them the illusion of safety.

In principle, it is perfectly easy to determine when and how it all started. It was when instead of thinking music, the composer started to think *about* music. There is no harm in that, so long as there is something to think about — so long as the composer has thought, invented music in the first place, and proceeds to think about it. And by 'music' I don't mean anything elaborate or complex: a tune, a little motif may have occurred to a composer, and he may proceed to think about it, about its character, its harmonic implications, its thematic possibilities and, yes, its constituent intervals, which might indeed prompt him to interpret the motif serially.

If, on the other hand, he thinks about it before it exists, and if, therefore, he reflects upon its constitution, its elements, before they have given rise to an audible entity, he runs the risk of thinking extra-musically, of thinking about things whose existence is visible, but not audible — and let us not forget that in our present state of uncertainty, many a mind which, constitutionally, belongs on this side of the iron curtain may well feel tempted to defect to the other side in order to partake of the safety of thought about music, in the illusory hope that such thought might, eventually, produce music. But that is he and now; we have not yet completed our answer to the question when and how it all started. If, at this point, I enlist the help of philosophy, it is not in order to obscure what, essentially, must remain a simple question, but, on the contrary, in order to simplify a state of creative affairs which, until now, has been obscured even by the most conscientious and the most musical thinkers.

A great deal has happened to philosophy since Kant's *Critique of Pure Reason*, but the beautiful truth of its gigantic corner-stones remains, I submit, unharmed. Let us translate his 'categories of thought' into simple language: it is as true today as it was when he first thought of the fact that it is impossible for us to imagine anything outside the dimensions of time and/or space. Just think of something, anything: it cannot be spaceless and timeless. Now, so far as music is concerned, the indispensable dimension is time and, hence, rhythm: it is impossible to think of any music, any snatch of a tune, any harmony even, outside time. So far as harmony is concerned, you may object: thinking of a dominant seventh's resolution to the tonic, you might say, you aren't concerned with its rhythm, but exclusively with this logical succession of chords, the establishment of harmonic tension and its expected resolution. True enough, but it is a *succession* of chords that defines, therefore, its harmonic rhythm, outside which you can't auralize the event; for it is an event and hence needs time in order to materialize, however mentally. And even if you invent a single chord, it will not only sound a beginning and an end but, if it *is* an invention, imply something preceding and/or succeeding it which, again, will imply a process, harmonic rhythm.

Nor, sticking to our subject, need we worry about harmony at the moment, for what I am concerned with when completing my reply to the question when and how it first happened is, simply, melody. Melodic, or rather rhythmic invention is indeed the elemental creative act; strictly speaking, it is always rhythmic, for there is music without harmony and music without melody and music without both, but no music, no melody and no harmony without rhythm — which is just another way of saying that there is no music without time. I don't want to repeat myself, but I certainly want to repeat Stravinsky: '. . . I heard and composed a melodic-harmonic phrase. I certainly did not (and never do) begin with a purely serial idea and, in fact, when I began I did not know, or care, whether all twelve notes would be used. After I had written about half the first phrase I saw its serial pattern, however, and then perhaps I began to work towards that pattern.' Having thought music, he began to think about it, which was not what his alleged idol did — Webern. It was the method of the unconscious or pre-conscious idol, Schoenberg — technically speaking, not all that unconscious either, as witness his enthusiastic approval of my emphatically Schoenbergian analysis of his Dylan Thomas dirge. But Webern inverted Schoenberg's procedure: no doubt Schoenberg explained to him that the row was the basis of the piece and, theoretically preoccupied, did not add the all-important circumstance that this basis naturally derived from an invention, that a row as such did not, musically, exist. The row as such is, as it were, the Kantian thing in itself,* which we can't hear; as soon as we auralize it, we rhythmicize it. We can, of course, see it — translate it into space, whereupon it ceases to be the thing in itself and doesn't begin to be anything else, for you can't hear it. It is as simple as that: it all started with Webern, the first composer to think about music before thinking music — despite his profound musicianship which, amongst his heirs and successors, affected only profound musicians. Or the one profound musician amongst them?

It would, perhaps, be unfair on Marx to regard him as the father of the iron curtain and all that goes with it — of all the im-moralities and inhumanities the development of communism has yielded. In fact, so far as Marx's own personality is concerned, and while one can detect much misjudgement, it would be difficult to trace any immoral or uncultural motivation. Likewise, we mustn't blame Webern for what has happened not only in his name, but as a result of his replacing composition with pre-composition — a practice which, by now, is almost universal. His musical person-ality, his creativity and, last but first, his sheer musicality were strong enough to overcome — in the majority of creative instances if not always — the handicap which his unprecedented approach to composition had produced for himself — an approach which, however, seemed motivated in much the same way as it is now-adays, inspired, that is to say, by the fear of insecurity and the proportionate temptation the rules of the game offered. And so he applied the rules before there was anything to apply them to, thereby lending an inaudible aspect to the very audible substance of his work, an aspect of which the work of the inventor, or rather, the discoverer of the rules is altogether free. But then, the very fact that he discovered them, however unconsciously, the very fact that he first encountered them in their application to musical thought (including, of course, his own), made it all the easier for him to adhere to the absolute primacy of musical invention, of specific, characteristic musical thought, which was a clearly demonstrable function of his creative character, anyhow.

At the same time, Webern's introduction of pre-composition, of thought about music before any music had been

---

* In my submission, a mistranslation (of *das Ding an sich*) down the ages: it ought to be 'the thing as such'.

born, foreheard and, alas, fore*saw* a typically modern attitude to musical creation, an at least partial loss of spontaneity, of old-fashioned inspiration, which came to pervade even the safest regions on this side of the iron curtain. We must not forget that even a Benjamin Britten, surely one of the concretest and most spontaneous inventors of our time, experienced yet enough 'thought about' before those concrete ideas occurred to him to be able to say that in his head, he had more or less finished something, and 'only had to fill in the notes' — a statement which a Mozart or Beethoven would have met with total incomprehension, even though Beethoven himself seems to have introduced thought about music into the world of the creator. But invariably, it was thought about something that had happened, on however primitive a level: there were decades of thought about the initial, incredibly simple-minded version of the 'Joy' tune, for instance, thought about how to turn simple-mindedness into extreme simplicity.

The disconcerting question of Stravinsky's influence, at least his potential influence, on future generations of intense talent is becoming a little easier, for he was amongst the very few composers of his time who were utterly unaffected by soundless music, by thought about what had not yet been thought. It is precisely in the area of serial technique that the potential force of such a composing attitude cannot be overestimated — and, para-doxically, Stravinsky's Schoenbergian influence could, in this respect, produce more actuality, more real results amongst future composers than Schoenberg's own. For Schoenberg himself, through his discovery of the dodecaphonic rules and their logical definition, came to play, quite guiltlessly, a far more ambiguous role: the way he silently composed was soon forgotten (at least so far as the order of creative events was concerned), his application of the rules so well remembered that many a dutiful twelve-tone composer composed stricter twelve-tone music than Schoenberg ever did in his life; it was, after all, Webern himself who was the first, ominous victim of this misunderstanding of Schoenberg's approach to composition, which flowed from his unconditional loyalty to the primacy of concrete, rhythmic invention. The rhythmless, temporarily musicless row was invented with and by Webern: his first creative steps are a retrograde version of Schoenberg's – but unlike the tone-row's mirror forms, this one does untold harm to the basic idea!

Stravinsky, quite unbothered by the rules, in whose verbal articulation he didn't show the slightest interest, cannot possibly be misunderstood the way Schoenberg has been and still is; his serial technique, his music-making rows — or rather, his row-making music — will either be understood or met with utter, harmless incomprehension.

Such incomprehension would be harmless inasmuch as it could not result in a misrepresentation, misuse and, truly musically speaking, an abuse of Stravinsky's technique comparable to the abuse Schoenberg's own technique continues to suffer (especially when it is improved upon); but if composers' deafness to Stravinsky's own serial invention should become at all widespread, it would be symptomatic of the greatest harm musical history can do to itself — the admission of extra-musicality, and hence unmusicality, into the ranks of its creators who, after all, are the only possible guardians of musicality. If they fail, musical history as we know it must either come to an end, or at least go into hibernation, with the prospect of an arctic winter.

It is not my intention to paint a gruesome picture of the future of music, but since its gruesome present is scarcely appreciated, the proportionate dangers which the future harbours have to be outlined for the purpose of both therapy and prophylaxis — or, in plain language, of confining music to the musical, however illiterate musically, and keeping it from the unmusical, however literate musically.

For the difference between the reason why quite a few of Mozart's innovations were condemned to remaining a potential influence and the cause of the threatening mere potentiality of Stravinsky's influence is extreme, and explicable with brutal simplicity: in order to materialize, Mozart's influence needed a Mozartian ear — whereas Stravinsky's needs an ear. As a musical culture, we have indeed sunk so low that the act of spontaneous improvisation, previously a first-hand experience for the most insignificant composer as well as the most substantial, has grown into so secret a science that there is many a musical composer who has hardly ever been in touch with it and, worse, does not miss its absence.

'In the manner I have described in our previous conversation I heard and composed a melodic-harmonic phrase.' That is all I am talking about — the ability to hear something without prior intellectual machinations which are designed to justify whatever the composer will eventually allow himself to hear. In this respect, Stravinsky's habitual professions that he 'had it' all from Webern could not have been wider of the mark, for it was Webern's abstractly constructed tone-row which introduced the element of *a priori* justification into serial technique, whereas Schoenberg, however complex his theoretical reflections after the creative event, confined himself to hearing and composing a melodic-harmonic phrase when it came to that moment of self-convincing and hence persuasive invention which the typical contemporary composer, musical or not, does without. Justification, a pseudo-creative concept which would have been incomprehensible to Mozart, has taken the place of conviction and persuasion. What convinces and persuades, however, is the idea itself — whereas what justifies is something else. The unconvincing, indeed meaningless ideas are legion which derive their justification from a complexly constructed tone-row whose very complexity is a delusion, for the simple reason that you can't hear it.

Concretely speaking, then, it isn't so much the notated stages of Stravinsky's serial technique which, one hopes against hope, will find a creative ear or two that will continue his music-making, as that which precedes his application of the technique, that to which the technique is applied, that which, in the case of each individual work, gives birth to its technique — the 'melodic-harmonic phrase' whose 'serial pattern' is discovered *a posteriori*. One has to be in close and constant contact with contemporary composing minds in order to appreciate that as pseudo-creative things stand at the moment, a shatteringly extended moment, the aforementioned typical composer of our undeveloping age needs almost super-human courage for the mere, sheer purpose of having an idea. It was this purpose which Hans Pfitzner threw into relief in his famous controversy with Alban Berg: he suggested that the new, atonal school had replaced the (untranslatable) *Einfall** with constructivism. How unfair he was to Schoenberg! And how unfair the Schoenbergians were to him! For so far as the Webernite tone-row is concerned, which in due course was to become all too

---

* 'A sudden idea', 'a spontaneous notion' would be the closest translation.

prototypical, a paradigm for every twelve-toner who lacked invention (and, alas, not only for him), Pfitzner's allegedly outmoded, old-fashioned tirade has retained its dynamic topicality down the decades, for almost three quarters of a century. But about Stravinsky's serialism he would have been just as wrong as he was about Schoenberg's. Ironically, therefore, one would have to explain Stravinsky's serialism in terms of Pfitzner's anti-serialism in order to define its potential influence on a future which, without it, will hardly deserve to be differentiated from the present: so long as the way back and forward to music-making is not found, we are not really entitled to talk of a 'future' at all; that shatteringly extended moment is in the process of proving itself a wellnigh infinite present.

About the crucial importance of the music-maker's future there is no doubt: it is a matter of life and death; and future ears, if any, hold his future in their hands. The mixed metaphor is purposive: too many are the hands nowadays which are not ears' hands. It has to be admitted, of course, that handed ears do still exist, but as well as being in a frightening minority, they only include one or two that have remained wholly uncorrupted by what happens on the other side of the iron curtain; in the serial world, perhaps not even one or two. The conclusion at which we arrived at the end of Chapter I now seems substantiated and can be confirmed with factual, indeed empirical assurance: 'Look after the physical reality of your music, he tells them, and the spirit will look after itself'.

IV. THE UNANSWERED QUESTION

In addition to the two questions we have tried to answer, there is one which seems destined to remain unanswered in our time, and compared to which those two are child's play. It is, nevertheless, a question which we cannot allow ourselves to escape — the less so since in the case of the great composers of the past, the answer is, in principle, available, and has, in fact, been given in quite a few instances; Thomas Mann, for example, answered it in respect of Wagner, and Adorno even attempted an answer in the case of Schoenberg. He thought he had answered it in respect of Stravinsky, too, but that alleged death-mask evaded it, denying Stravinsky creative substance. The question, then, is what Stravinsky's music conveys; what those of us who understand it are puzzled by is not only his creative character, which we have tried to shed light on, but also the character of the creations themselves, that which distinguishes them from any other major creative output.

We are moving dangerously near a fallacious question which, according to Hugo Cole, lies 'beyond the questions "How is music constructed? How is music shaped by context?"' He describes it as 'the ultimate, never-to-be-answered question', but fails to realize that as he and everybody else puts it, it is wrong: '"What is music about?" In Bach's case at least, many would agree that behind the notes there is something exalted, supremely ordered, akin to the universal. The listener who, in answer to a questionnaire of Vernon Lee's, wrote "Bach is Angels and tops of trees and mountains" spoke, naively, for us all.'

Speak for yourselves, thank you very much. Never in what I claim is my understanding experience of Bach's music have angels, tops of trees, or mountains played the remotest role, nor indeed do angels and tops of trees occur in my mental life, while mountains mean skiing to me and, admittedly, pocket-score-reading on the way up in the lift. I am not being flippant: the fallacy lies in the implication of the mere possibility of a simile, or similes. Messrs Lee and Cole are suggesting that what Bach's music expresses also finds its way into our consciousness through our experience of certain symbols and/or divine messengers. And they miss precisely that which the question claims to be about: what tops of trees and mountains (if not angels) tell us comes, exclusively, from within us; what Bach tells us comes from him. The ineluctable implication that we project meaning on to Bach as we project meaning on to tops of trees and mountains is really the supreme act of arrogance, ignoring as it does that which we could never have experienced without Bach, because he introduced us to it, discovered it for us.

'Something exalted, supremely ordered, akin to the universal' behaves a little more respectfully toward the discoveries in which Bach lets us participate, and cannot, in fact, be called fallacious — but merely irrelevant: there are plenty of things, utterly unrelated to, and dissimilar from, music, to which that 'something' is equally relevant, higher mathematics for instance. Stravinsky himself would have answered that ultimate question quite logically: 'Nothing.' He did, after all, tell us that his music didn't express anything — a remark which has been misunderstood from the word 'express'. For what he implied was, quite obviously, that his music did not convey any of those things which we spontaneously regard as expressible; programme music does, and essentially, Stravinsky characterized his own music by way of a negative definition: it was not concerned with extra-musical life. Nor, for that matter, is Bach's, even where he uses extra-musical life towards structuring his pure music, however impure such formal assistance.

As soon as we say that x is 'about' y, we imply that x narrates, or ponders, or expresses, or explains, or elucidates, feelings about — but what in any case makes us more closely aware of — y. The further implication is that y is namable; we have, in fact, named it. If, on the other hand, the question is 'never to be answered', how can it be posed; or if it is posed, why can't it ever be answered? What, in other words, does it mean, and what is the rejoinder to my claim that in the circumstances as just defined, it is meaningless? 'About' implies conceptual thought, or a musical imitation of conceptual thought, such as the telling of a story through music.

So long as we cling to conceptual thought as the only means of realizing truth, in the sense of both conceiving and presenting it as real, so long as we don't realize that there are truths inaccessible to conceptual thought altogether but accessible to musical thought, as well as truths whose understanding is exclusively musical, although verbal thought can refer, allude to them, establish associations with them, we shall never get anywhere near a conceptual understanding of musical understanding. As children, we had to grow up verbally, which is why we make words the ultimate arbiter. If one allowed a highly musical child's mind to develop, in the first place, musically, this unique member of humanity, once fully developed, could teach us a thing or two about the inadequacy of conceptual as opposed to musical insight. In the history of humanity, Mozart's seems to have been the only mind which, spontaneously and unconditionally, clung to musical thought as the primary source of perception and understanding.

Perception? A theory of cognition which took musical cognition into account would have to accept the fact that without a —

primarily emotional — *experience* of any given music, its perception, and hence its understanding, cannot take place. The truth it has to tell has to be experienced in order to be recognized: *it is cognized emotionally and can then be recognized intellectually* — analytically, for instance, though still not through words, but rather through what we did in our complete music example from the Dylan Thomas dirge.

Whether answerable or not, the question of what music is about had better be left alone in the circumstances — which, if their musicality is remembered and fully retained, do not allow us, we have just noted, to think in terms of 'about' anyway. However, the question, not of what Stravinsky's music is about, but of its character, of what distinguishes it from anybody else's music, we can at least investigate along the conceptual lines that have proved helpful in the case of other composers; though we may not be able to answer it, we might at least contribute the first steps towards an answer.

Wagner we accept, instinctively, as Stravinsky's opposite, the expressionist *par excellence* as opposed to the one and only suppressionist. Yet there is one negative trait which the two share — and exclusively, too: they seem to be the only great composers who arouse violent hostility in highly musical musicians. In the case of Wagner's music, I consider such reactions inevitable — and here I am going beyond what other thinkers, such as Thomas Mann and, incidentally, Adorno too, have found out about the nature of his music. For the likely fact is that Wagner's inspirations make us identify with feelings which we experience as bad, evil; and that there are those amongst us who can't forgive him, who blame him for having corrupted them, however temporarily — for the duration of a performance. But without *experiencing* these feelings, we cannot understand their psychological truth: it was Wagner's artistic duty to convey his psychological discoveries through the persuasiveness of his music. The shady side of *any* Wagnerian figure in his mythological world offers us confirmatory verbal thought which refers, alludes to those evil feelings, which establishes convincing conceptual associations with them.

I personally have no doubt that on top of it all, Wagner's music conveys truths altogether inaccessible to conceptual thought, and for which we only have empty words, such as 'metaphysics'. And the very combination, the amalgam of evil and the nameless, the other world, the timeless and spaceless we can't conceptually grasp, is too much for some of us to bear — for the most violent of the Wagner-haters and Wagner-baiters.

No, there is no need to remind me that this is not a book about Wagner — for in an exact negative way it is. Wordlessly speaking, that is to say, I give it as my deeply — unconceptually — considered opinion that the polarity between Stravinsky and Schoenberg (some of which we have seen crumble, anyway) is as nothing compared to the polarity between Stravinsky and Wagner: Stravinsky's music is experienced as the precise negative of Wagner's: it suppresses what Wagner's expresses, without leaving any doubt about the concrete, musically palpable and tangible nature of what it suppresses. Clinically, it is of the greatest significance to observe that the most passionate Stravinsky-lovers one knows are, at the same time, the most conscientious — invariably moralizing — objectors to Wagner's music.

Is the implication, then, that what is felt to be evil is amalgamated with the nameless* in Stravinsky's music, too? My answer is not only the *Symphony of Psalms* but also, well above all, his sovereign *Mass* — to which, instructively enough, many a musical believer in the mass as such passionately objects: that which he rightly expects from music is being suppressed in the most religious of religious compositions, of all works? Aphoristically, maybe, meaningless words can assume, or at least borrow meaning: Wagner's music offends by turning us evil, whereas Stravinsky's offends by not turning us good.

But that's not the end of the hostile story about Stravinsky's music. Brahms and Webern, when they fail to be as expressive as they want to be, and when their music is therefore open to centrally relevant criticism, are never blamed for their inhibitions: so far as I am aware, I was the first to diagnose them. No, people love these masters' music the more for its neurotic shortcomings, for they are able to identify with the all too human inhibitions which thus manifest themselves. What a relief that the creators of such great music are human after all, what utter relief that the music itself is, sharing as it does the admiring listener's most embarrassing traits — his shyness, his blushes, his occasional

---

*For a pious Jew, God is nameless, in that his (Hebrew) name must not be enunciated; a different word is substituted. The present writer, an unpious Jew, approves, so long as it is agreed that musically, this nameless truth is closely definable.

unwillingness to face his own emotions! Stravinsky, on the other hand, faces them all, faces things of which we hadn't even been aware before he told us about — 'about'? no: before he winkingly insinuated — their ill-repressed existence in our own minds. Small wonder that there are those amongst us who won't have it, won't tolerate such superhuman control over clearly acknowledged, elementally powerful feelings, won't accept the mere possibility of such supreme balance between that which is being suppressed and its open-eared suppression! For in order for the suppression to succeed, there must be at least as much natural power behind it as behind the suppressed material itself. Where the music of Brahms and Webern can't get it out (how understandable! how disarming!), Stravinsky's can — but, for the first time in the history of the art, won't. With passionate detachment, it exposes force and counter-force, and counter-forces all those elemental forces to a halt: the apparent staticism thus achieved is the result of opposing, extreme dynamisms.

It is for this reason that Stravinsky's music is not developmental: in it, development is not arrested, but successfully opposed — frontally attacked; its anti-developments are, specifically, traceable. They avail themselves, at their maturest stages, of twelve-tone technique — the developmental technique *par excellence* turned in upon itself. Now, once that inescapable control which is the character of Stravinsky's message, or anti-message, has been traced in concrete, analytic detail, our unanswered question will have been fully answered. Meanwhile, let us confess that if his kind of inexpressive expression, this overwhelmingly expressive anti-*espressivo* hadn't happened, we would have been able to show, on the basis of our entire history of music, that it couldn't possibly happen: all genius is unique, but this one is the uniquest of the lot.

PART TWO

STRAVINSKY SEEN

Cocteau

To Miss Cosman
my compliments

I Strawnzy
London Nov 6/59

A NOTE ON THE ILLUSTRATIONS

So far as Stravinsky at work was concerned, all drawings in this book were done at rehearsals for BBC concerts he conducted in 1958, 1959, and 1961. They included a concert performance of *Oedipus Rex* in 1959, in which Cocteau took the part of the Speaker; hence, and because of his long association with the composer, his presence. The sketches of Stravinsky in tails were done on his very last visit to London in September, 1965, at the Royal Festival Hall, where he conducted part of a concert of his music. I have allowed myself to transfer his inscription from one drawing to another — for purely spatial reasons. I may add that I was far too shy to show him the drawings, having been intent throughout upon drawing him behind his back, metaphorically as well as literally; it was Elizabeth Lutyens who insisted on showing them to him: hence the inscription. The two etchings — one introducing Part Two, the other at the very end of the book — were, of course, made subsequently, in 1981.

Milein Cosman

INDEX